MOON PHASES
INTRODUCTION TO THE NIGHT SKY
Science & Technology
Teaching Edition

SPEEDY
PUBLISHING

Speedy Publishing LLC
40 E. Main St. #1156
Newark, DE 19711
www.speedypublishing.com

Copyright 2015

The Moon takes 27 days, 7 hours, 43 minutes, 11.6 seconds to go all the way around the Earth.

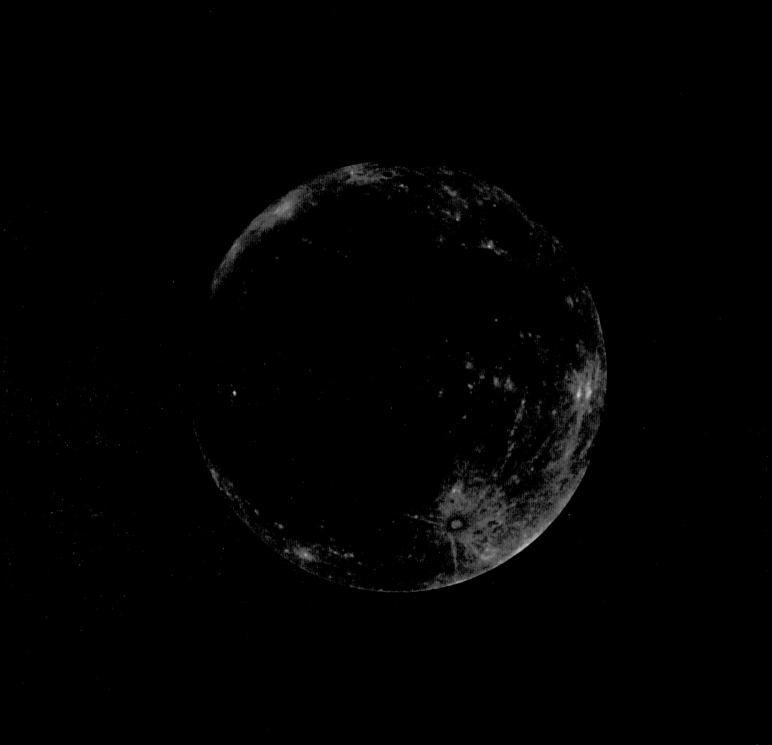

A new moon is the side of
the moon facing the Earth is
not illuminated.
The new moon phase occurs
when the Moon is directly
between the Earth and Sun.

FACT

The surface of the Moon features a huge number of impact craters from comets and asteroids that have collided with the surface over time.

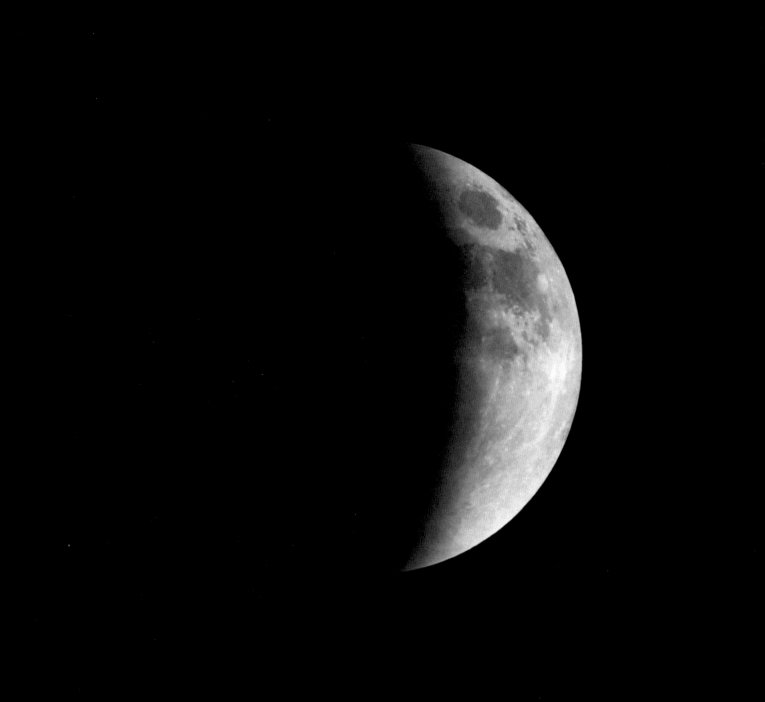

A waxing crescent moon is
when the Moon looks like
crescent and the crescent
increases in size from
one day to the next.

FACT

The Moon is very hot during the day but very cold at night.

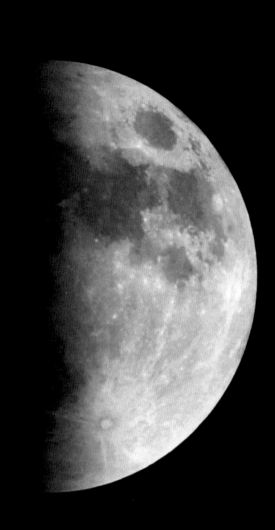

During first quarter, 1/2
of the lit portion of the
moon is visible for the
first half of the evening.

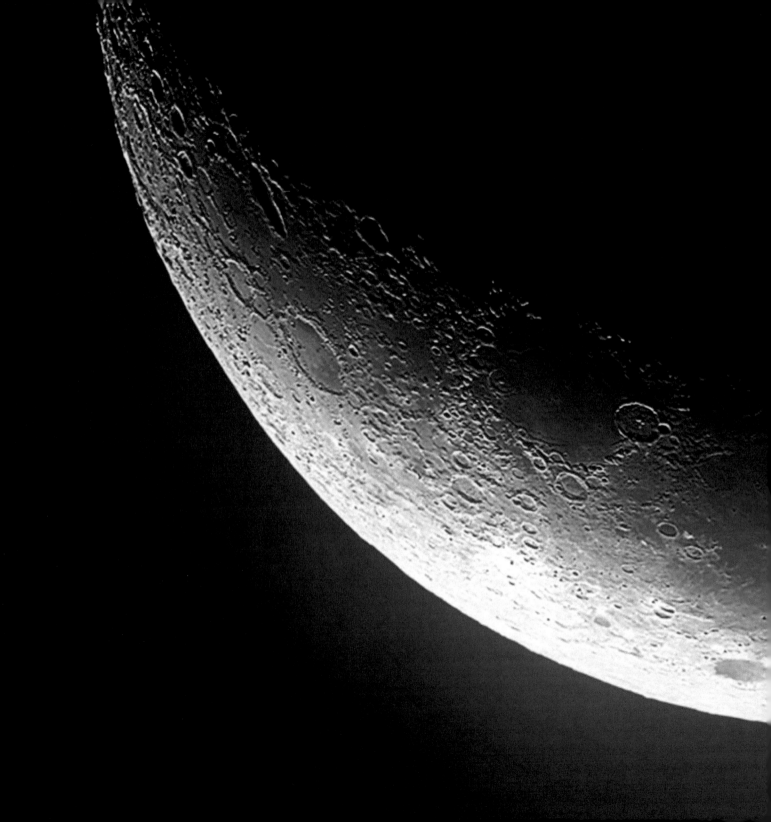

FACT

The Moon is the Earth's only natural satellite.

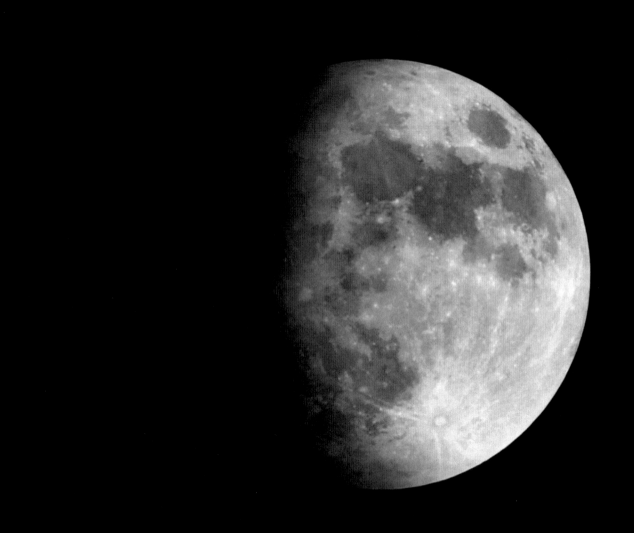

A waxing gibbous moon occurs when more than half of the lit portion of the Moon can be seen. The Moon remains in the sky most of the night.

FACT

Only 59% of the moon's surface is visible from earth.

A full moon is when we can observe the entire lit portion of the Moon. The full moon phase occurs when the Moon is on the opposite side of the Earth from the Sun.

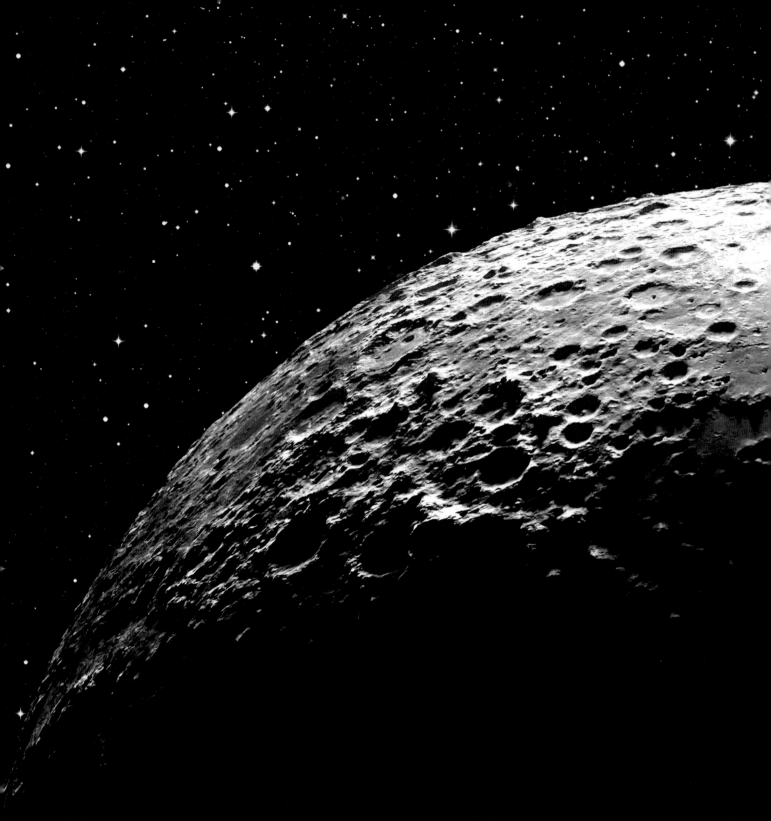

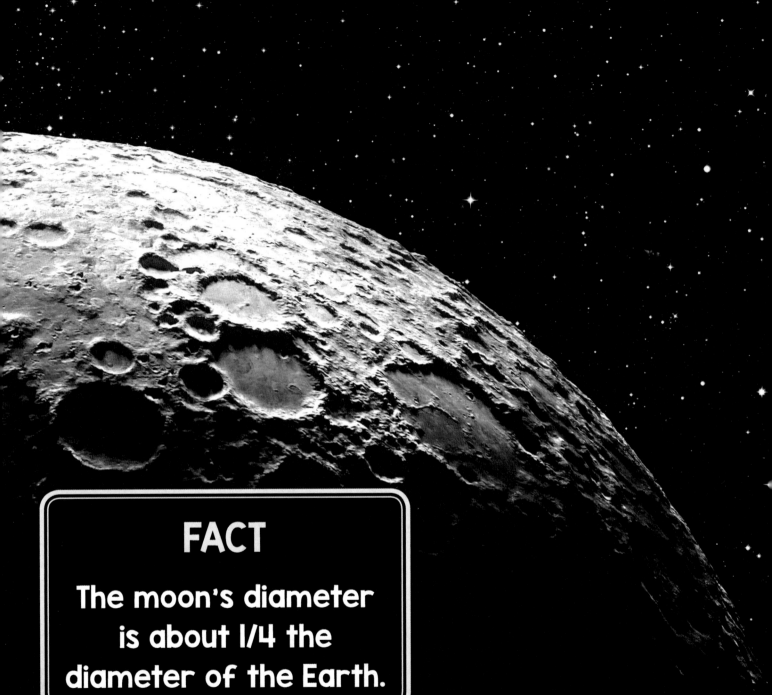

FACT

The moon's diameter is about 1/4 the diameter of the Earth.

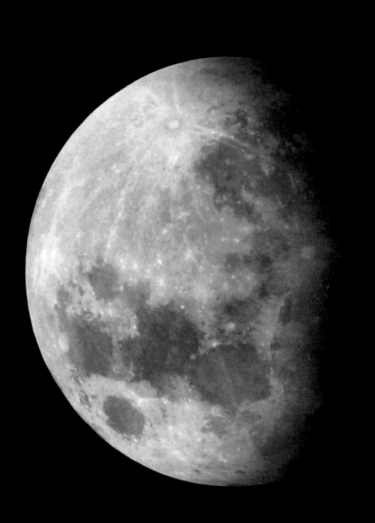

A waning gibbous moon occurs when more than half of the lit portion of the Moon can be seen and the shape decreases in size from one day to the next.

FACT

The moon is the only extraterrestrial body that has ever been visited by humans.

The last quarter moon is
when half of the lit portion
of the Moon is visible after
the waning gibbous phase.

FACT

The rise and fall of the tides on Earth is caused by the Moon.

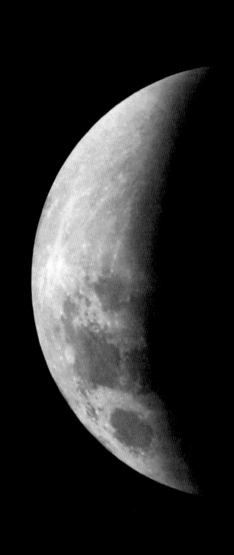

A waning crescent moon is when the Moon looks like the crescent and the crescent decreases in size from one day to the next.

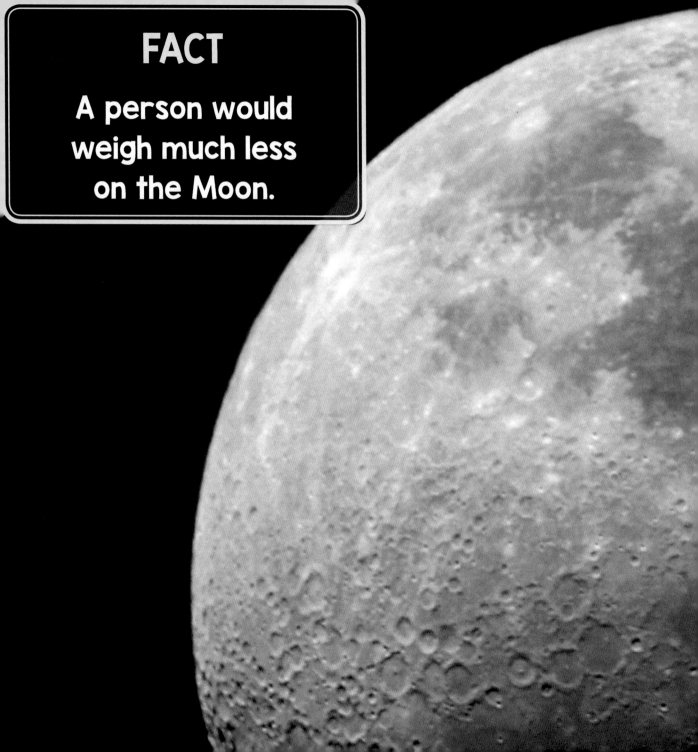

FACT

A person would weigh much less on the Moon.

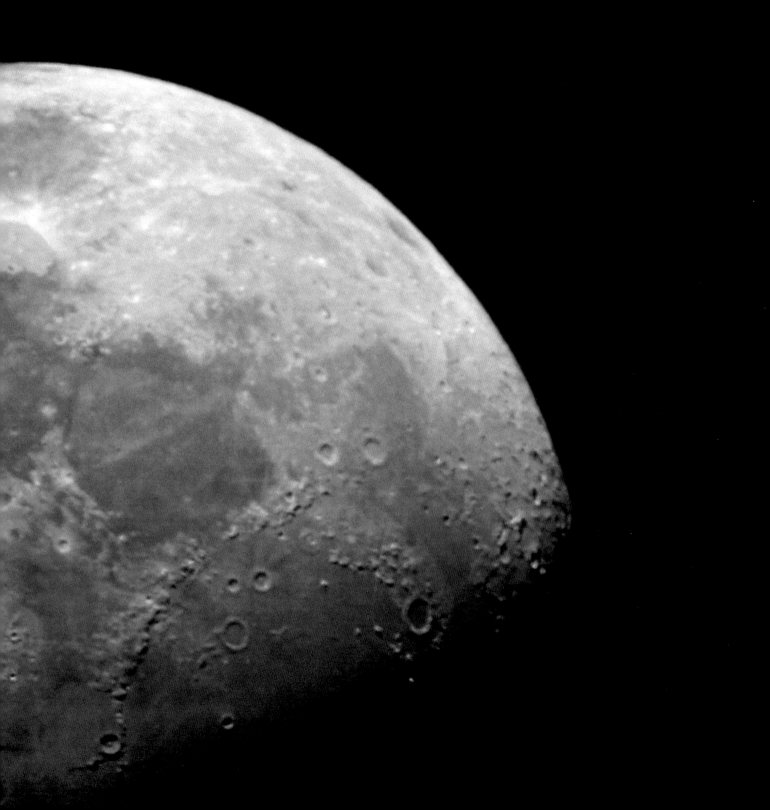

FACT

The surface area of
the moon is 14,658,000
square miles.

FACT

When a month has two full moons, the second full moon is called a blue moon.

Made in United States
Orlando, FL
02 June 2023